Words I Use

In My School

Victoria Huseby

FRANKLIN WATTS
LONDON · SYDNEY

First published in 2005 by
Franklin Watts
96 Leonard Street
London
EC2A 4XD

Franklin Watts Australia
Level 17, 207 Kent Street
Sydney, NSW 2000

Editor: Rachel Tonkin
Series design: Mo Choy
Art director: Jonathan Hair
Photography: Chris Fairclough
Literacy consultant: Gill Matthews

The publisher wishes to thank Years 4, 5 and 6 of
Streatham Wells Primary School for agreeing to appear in this book.

With thanks to Slade Green Infant School
for the photograph on pages 20 and 21.

A CIP catalogue record for this book is
available from the British Library

ISBN: 0 7496 6086 4

Dewey classification: 371

Printed in China

Contents

About this book
This book helps children to learn key words in the context of when and where they are used. Each picture is described in the main text, and the words in bold are labelled on the picture along with other key words, as a starting point for discussion. The open-ended questions will also help with language development. On pages 22-23 a simple quiz encourages children to look again in detail at all the pictures in the book, and this can be used to develop referencing skills.

display board

hat

coat

In the corridor

When you arrive at school, you hang up your **coat** and **schoolbag** on a **coat hook**. People pin messages and **pictures** on the **display board**.

What do you have in your school corridor?

noticeboard

workbooks

chair

drawers

whiteboard

globe

table

bin

le bricks

lydron

ego

ego

ego

In the classroom

The classroom is where you have lessons. The teacher writes on the **whiteboard**. You put things in the **drawers** to help keep the classroom tidy.

?

What else helps to keep this classroom tidy?

glue stick

pencils

sticky tape

felt-tip pens

pencil sharpener

paper

pencil case

scissors

An art lesson

These children are making patterns. They are using **pencils**, **felt-tip pens**, and a **glue stick** or **sticky tape** to stick things down.

?

What other things are the children using?

gate

bench

friends

In the playground

During break time at school, you play with your **friends** in the playground. Children at this school can play a **game** or sit on the **bench**. The **teacher** watches over everyone.

What games do you play at break time?

lunch box

fork

plate

spoon

banana

drink carton

water jug

apple

table

bowl

beaker

Lunch time

Everyone eats lunch together at a **table** in the school hall. Some children bring their lunch in a **lunch box**. Others eat school dinners.

?

What do you like to have for your lunch?

In a music lesson

These children are practising a tune together. They each play a musical instrument. One of them shakes some **maracas**. Another hits a **tambourine**.

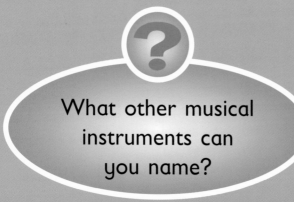

?

What other musical instruments can you name?

sleigh bells

violin

maracas

wooden block

violin bow

recorder

tambourine

videos

shelf

chair

page

rug

16

bookcase

books

book box

Choosing a book

In the school library there are lots of **books** to read. You look on the **shelves** to find the book you want. You can sit on the **chair** to read it.

What sort of books do you like to read?

Using a computer

A **computer** has a **keyboard**, a **screen** and a **mouse**. You can put a **disk** or **CD** into the computer. You can listen to instructions on the computer with **headphones**.

When do you use a computer?

computer

headphones

printer

screen

disk

CD

mouse

keyboard

Going home

Children are collected from school by a **parent** or another adult. The **caretaker** clears up and looks after the school after the children have left.

?

What does the caretaker do in your school?

roof

caretaker

plant

school

tree

door

parent

window

playground

Can you spot . . . ?

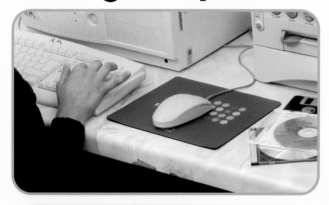

A computer mouse.

A drink carton.

A noticeboard.

A pair of scissors.

A pencil case.

A plant.

A plate.

A recorder.

A roll of sticky tape.

A schoolbag.

A tambourine.

A woolly hat.

Index